BROOKE'S 101 TOP SECRETS

This is a work of ideas, products, and concepts of the author's imagination. Any resemblance to actual person's ideas, products, and concepts are entirely coincidental.

© 2018 Brooke Gantt

All rights reserved.

No part of this book may be reproduced or stored in a retrieval system, or transmitted in any form or by any means, electronic, mechanical, photocopying, recording, or otherwise, without written permission from the author. For information, contact www.BuysB.Global

WBM Publishing

ISBN-13: 978-1-490-51434-5

BROOKE'S 101 TOP SECRETS

Brooke Gantt

Table of Contents

Are You a Leader? 1-4

Opportunities to Make Money & Be Your Own Boss 4-14

Amazing Million $ Ideas 15-19

38 Ways to Make Money Writing 20-22

Secrets to Help Someone Else Feel Rich 23-25

21 Job & Home-Based Ideas 26-27

More Ways to Make Money 28

Opportunities for Children to Earn Money 29

Bonus: Money Secrets 30-31

Decorating Tips 32

How to Fulfill Your Purpose………........................……… 33

Most People Do Not Want to Tell Others Their Secrets, but Brooke is Sharing Hers With You! But First Read the Information Below!!!

Are You a Leader?

YES, you demonstrated leadership when you selected this guide. You are on the road to literally becoming the mover and shaker you always desired to be.

Brooke Gantt has been featured in the hottest magazines in the world (Seventeen, Glamour, Allure), graced the runways at the most exclusive fashion shows (Versace, Tommy Hilfiger, Neiman Marcus), and appeared in numerous commercials (Macy's, Target, Levi's), and television programs (Good Morning America, The View, The Today Show). Brooke recognized the opportunity to help people reach their highest potential through *Brooke's 101 Top Secrets and* her company called *BusyB.Global – Finding Your Purpose, Mate, & Wealth*. Everyone has a unique mission on earth; this mission is to realize who you are, be over comers and not opt to live life without direction.

Have you ever had an idea and didn't act on it, but then down the road you saw someone else doing the same idea you thought of? I have! And most of us have been there too, but now you have the opportunity to act on an idea and follow through with it.

This guide contains powerful and creative business ideas, career opportunities, and as a bonus, money secrets that may be of genuine interest to you. Some ideas were gleamed from discussions with family and friends. Many dreamed up in the shower, during the night, and in long-haul flights. Most have been tested, modified, adapted, and refined. However, we cannot guarantee success for anybody, but we will get you on the right track.

Leaders Come in Many Different Forms

Let's discover what your leadership style is. Go to http://psychology.about.com/library/quiz/bl-leadershipquiz.htm to answer some vital questions.

Your answers will help you determine which business is compatible with your personal skills and ambitions. The second step is to seek out your gifts, talents, and purpose.

Ask yourself these three simple questions:

- What hobbies caught your attention as a child?
- Is there a job that you would work without getting paid for it?
- If you had a million dollars today what company would you open?

Those three questions will help determine your gifts and what you aspire to be. Your talents are God given.

- What are you good at? It could be cooking, dancing, acting, teaching, sewing, calculating, speaking, or writing, just to name a few.
- How can you improve on it? Is it taking a class and/or practicing?

Your purpose in life is also spiritual and requires prayer and God's meditation. But please keep in mind that everyone seems to think that their purpose has to be something huge. It may not be something huge; it may be something as simple as blessing your coworker or family member with a hug, service, a gift, affirmation, or quality time.

Once you figured out the enormous power you have within I urge you to choose the idea(s) that cater to your gifts and talents and then line it up with your purpose. I would love to conquer every idea that comes to my mind. The reality is you want to stay focused on your strengths and enjoy every moment while you earn cash income and become successful... you never know, we could see you on *Good Morning America* telling your story.

Lifestyle

At this point, we wish to remind you that money is not the most important element in our lives and without family and taking care of yourself we are poor. Inside this guide you will also find lifestyle ideas on intimacy, decorating, cooking, spirituality, organizing special events such as birthdays, and other subjects that will stimulate and help make you an all-around better person.

Please be aware that our information offers only product, personal, or service ideas. The rest is up to you!

In closing, we would love to hear your success stories. Please keep in touch and contact us at www.BusyB.Gobal/journeys. Otherwise, we wish the best for you in all your endeavors.

"Life is easy when you know your purpose." *Brooke*

Blessings!

Opportunities to Make Money & Be Your Own Boss

Own an Innovative & Groundbreaking Modeling/One-Stop Shop Agency

Help young talent become professional models and be the best they can be by including these few creative ideas in your business proposal: (1) Upload portfolios and personality videos to the model's tablet, such as an iPad to show to clients. (2) Have your models dressed to help them stand out during castings such as a slim fitted white jacket with the name of your agency on the back. (3) Provide health insurance. (4) Build a wardrobe, accessory, and toilettes closet for talent to have access to for castings. (5) Create an auctioning section on your website to allow clients to bid on a model for specific jobs. The "eBay" of modeling.

Captivating Gifts for Teenagers - Earn Cash While You Create Powerful Gifts to Help Others Build Confidence

At the present time, there are countless uninformed young adults who suffer from low self-esteem. Based on daily experience, people's feelings and thoughts about themselves fluctuate. From a teenager's standpoint, how their friends treat them, a grade they receive on an exam, and ups and downs in a romantic relationship all contribute to their confidence.

If people know who they are, normal "ups and downs" may be temporary fluctuations in how they feel about themselves. On the other hand, for people who don't know who they are these "ups and downs" can make all the difference in the world.

If you would like to be in a business where you can help teens build their confidence this is perfect for you. Fill a basket with self-esteem gifts. Include inspirational books, "I'm Special" or "I'm Smart" bathroom or bedroom mirror magnets you can create with a sharpie, small shaped colorful laminated paper, glue, and magnet pieces to remind them every morning who they are. This unique and beautiful gift will surely help young adults feel good about themselves and a perfect way to make cash income.

Create Your Own Exclusive Natural Hair and Skin Products – Turn Your Love for Healthy Hair and

Skin into Money! Carol's Daughter has done it successfully for years!

There are various hair and skin products on the market that contain harmful chemicals. Produce fast and easy natural hair and skin products in the comfort of your own home and earn a good income. No special skills are necessary to operate this business. As long as you have the ambition to follow simple instructions and care about hair and skin, you'll be on the road toward lifelong income.

Two great books to read are *Grow Hair in 12 Weeks* and *Grow Hair and Stop Hair Loss* by Riquette Hofstein. Now you will have access to hair and skin care ingredients, such as herbs and other special remedies. The products are affordable and easy to make.

Making Thousands Writing & Selling Your Books

Become an Author Today - Want to become an author but don't have a title or concept? Read some of these ideas to get your juices flowing:

1. **Title:** Stepping Stones

    Cover: Bare Feet Stepping on Stones

    Genre: Business

    Concept: 12 Steps to a Successful Business

2. **Title:** Lock Him Up and Throw Away the Key

    Cover: Hot Male Model Locked Behind Bars

Genre: Comedy

Concept: Fun & hilarious short story with pictures about what it would be like to have a guy locked up behind bars serving a life sentence so that he can't cheat on his girlfriend. Create an image in the reader's mind of the girlfriend knowing where her guy is at all times. Be creative and write about the benefits of locking up your man and throwing away the key!

3. **Title:** Seven Deadly Jezebels

   Cover: Beautiful Mystical Woman

   Genre: Drama

   Concept: Think of seven people in your life that have caused chaos, division, destruction, etc. Explain how these people have affected your life and how you overcame it. This could be written as a fiction or non-fiction story.

These examples are unique and simple to write about.

Make up to $273,000 in 11 months and Own a Rare Online Traveling Company

Despite the economy today, millions of people travel around the world. To take part in this traveling business is based upon asking yourself three simple questions: (1) Would you like to own a fully functional creative customized traveling company? (2) Do you have good organization skills or know someone that does? (3) Do you have 130 dollars to invest? If someone asked you these three questions, what would be YOUR responses? If you can answer "yes" to the above questions, then you are in the position to create both cash income and your own traveling company in seconds! Who are traveling moguls? Well, look in the mirror, friend. For further information please visit www.BusyB.Global.

Earn Up to $5,000 Per Month Selling a Popular Accessory – Watch it Charm® is a true ground floor opportunity. Females from around the world can wear it in style. Hundreds of designs can be created by you. All you need is a pocket watch with a chain and a few charms. Wrap the chain around your wrist and say to yourself, "Why didn't I think of that?" Watch manufacturers are already making a fortune marketing watches to a niche market, which just keeps growing and growing. Why not get in on the action with this unique style?

TOP SECRET: Sell Clothes & Accessories for Profit! Poshmark, Mercari, and eBay are simple and fun ways to buy and sell fashion – straight from your smartphone. Your family and friends will ask you, "Where did you get that from?" or "What are you doing for extra cash or is it Top Secret?" Download the apps today and have fun dazzling the people you know or start earning money immediately.

Create and Development a Stress-Free Harmonious Home – There is nothing better in the world then to come home to a stress-free environment especially for returning soldiers from war or females who were victims of sex trafficking. This is your time to give back and help someone else feel at home, safe, and relaxed. Be creative and organize activities to help girls with their confidence and self-image or help soldiers cope with everyday living again. What the secret to be financially successful in this business? Apply for grants and start today!

A Love Gift – For someone special!

This gift is filled with love. You will never guess with what. Purchase cut-out letters of the alphabet, twenty-seven gift bags, tissue paper, and ribbon. Use the person's favorite colors. Grab one bag and place the letter "A" on the front of the bag and then stuff the bag with tissue paper. Place the desired item that begins with the letter "A" in the bag. For instance, if the person likes apples, put an apple in the bag. After that grab another bag and glue the letter "B" on the front of the bag. Continue this process until you have finished the entire alphabet.

To make it simple, spell out the person's name instead of using the entire alphabet and use the same concept. Great gift for under the Christmas tree, a baby shower, or birthday gift.

These days, people do not have time to shop for the items needed for this gift. Take the time out and charge a fee to shop for the items. Your client list could consist of family, friends, and colleagues.

How to Express the SECRECT POWER Inside of Your Creative Moment - The best way to show your family you care is to take the time to show it through food.

For Dinner Time:

Prepare meals from different parts of the world to change up the menu.

For instance, on Mondays fix a dinner from India. On Tuesdays cook a dinner from Africa, Wednesdays prepare it from Mexico, Thursdays fix Japanese, Fridays go out to eat at a restaurant, Saturdays; if you live near New York City take a train to the city, just for lunch and return home that same day, and Sundays have a traditional American dinner, for instance: mashed potatoes, fried chicken, hamburgers, or make it a seafood night.

Don't want to prepare food every day? You could also cook everything on Sunday for the week. Purchase nice food savers like chefs do to keep the food fresh and easy to get to for meals and snacks.

Prepare these meals for couples and families and make a profit.

Amazing Million $ Ideas

Secrets to Earning Income in the Beauty Industry

Braiding hair, sew in weaves, or owning a hair salon are the best and most profitable ways to earn money in the hair industry. Whether you do hair in a salon or in your basement legally, set yourself apart from the masses by offering groundbreaking secrets. For further information about the ideas please visit www.BusyB.Global.

Make Millions Investing in an Inventive Weight Loss Product - Have the funds, the resources, and the motivation to research? Help design a new weight loss product that can make diets and workouts obsolete. This product will improve all body types without the use of will power, the need to count calories, or change your whole lifestyle. The best part is that you won't have to exercise or get dangerous surgeries such as liposuction or a tummy tuck. What is the secret to weight loss? For further information about the product please visit www.BusyB.Global.

Produce Millions with the Best Kept Secret on the Planet - Everyone is familiar with the use of billboards, transit billboards, and posters. Why not take it to the next-level? This concept will generate very high spectator satisfaction and will represent clients with the integrity that each one desires and deserves.

How does it work? For further information about the concept please visit www.BusyB.Global.

Get Rich Helping Others Through Entertainment - Are you ready to change your life and the lives of our youngsters? Are you ready to make more money faster and in a way you never thought possible? Within everyone is a secret code that can be easily unlocked with the right guidance. Create a theatrical Broadway or off-Broadway musical that empowers, motivates, and builds confidence. Just ask yourself one question: Do you want the ready-to-perform lucrative script today? If yes, you are on the road to success. For further information about the script please visit www.BusyB.Global.

Develop a Fashion & Lifestyle Workshop Program/Modeling Contest! – Organize a week-long workshop program that caters to fashion for ages 13-18. Start out with an introduction to modeling and then have a runway, make-up & hair, and etiquette workshop. The last night will be the modeling contest where each will have the opportunity to walk in front of judges to potentially become a model. Would you like to know the money-making ideas that will help your modeling workshop and contest stand out? For further information about the ideas please visit www.BusyB.Global.

Festive Christmas in July/Slumber Party – Christmas in any month is always exciting, but yours will have an edge. Organize an event with Christmas decorations, music, and food, just a name a few ideas. Entertain the guests with games and several unique concepts that will help you make a profit and will make you say Merry Christmas! For further information about the ideas above please visit www.BusyB.Global.

Get Creative with Your Next Spellbinding Magazine – We will never get tired of information whether it's about fashion, dating, money, and news. Magazines can be very profitable for the people who promote and organize it. This magazine will have innovative ideas for either an online magazine or for the people who purchase magazines at the grocery store. This concept will blow your mind and you will be on your way to a successful money-making business. Can I get an Amen! For further information about the magazine ideas please visit www.BusyB.Global.

The Best of Both Worlds on Wheels — The gourmet trucking business is always looking for the next big food or dessert that will be a BIG hit on the streets. Well, why not open a truck of your own with an ingenious idea? As a bonus, we will unlock an additional secret for an awesome truck business. For further information about the ideas please visit www.BusyB.Global.

Writing, Journaling, Scrapbooking, Illustrating, Notetaking with a Twist! – This concept will help jumpstart a writer's career. Not a writer? This money-making idea can also be used for scrapbooking, illustrating, journaling, or notetaking. Make a profit today! For further information about the ideas please visit www.BusyB.Global.

> *"Your Attitude Determines Your Altitude."*
>
> *(Covey, 2005)*

38 Ways to Make Money Writing

Ever wanted to become a blogger or a writer for health magazines or www.ehow.com? Here are some engrossing ideas you could write about and make some cash…

19. Remedies for Smoother Skin

20. Hints to Reduce Breast Soreness

21. Problem-Free Nursing Ideas

22. Ways to Overcome Bad Breath

23. Cover-up Ideas for Bruises

24. Hints for Arriving Alert When Jet-Lagged

25. Ways to Fight Cellulite

26. Ways to Get Him to Say "I Do"

27. Tips to Stop the Dryness of Chapped Lips

28. Ways to Stay on the Low Side of Cholesterol

29. Remedies to Win the Battle of Colds

30. Ways to Smooth and Soothe Corns and Calluses

31. How to Beat Depression

32. Ways to Keep Diabetes Under Control

33. Tips to Ease Tension

Brooke's 101 Top Secrets

34. Ways to Make Your Parents Feel Extra Special

35. Ways to Deal with the Dark

36. Treatments for Minor Burns

37. Ways to Get the Kinks Out of Your Neck

38. Remedies to Beat the Flu Bug

39. Ways to Get a Clean Shave

40. How to Brighten Stained Teeth

41. Ways to Alleviate the Symptoms of Allergies

42. Ways to Deal with a Hangover

43. Hints to Take Away Headaches

44. Ways to Stay Symptom-Free of Menopause

45. Ways to Counteract Morning Sickness

46. Motion Sickness Cures

47. Ways to Perfect Posture

48. Treatments for Cats and Dogs

49. Skin-Soothing Remedies for Poison Ivy and Oak

50. Scriptures and a Prayer to Get to Heaven (Romans Road)

51. Cooling Treatments for Sunburn

52. Tips to Slow Aging and Wrinkles

53. Coping Measures for Phobias and Fears
54. Coping Tactics for Fever
55. Feet Treats for Foot and Back Aches
56. Ways to Keep Blood Pressure Under Control

Secrets to Help Someone Else Feel Rich

57. Pick a day to do fun things with your spouse. For instance, make every Tuesday a fun day. If you work during the day, make Tuesday evening's fun.

58. Use the same dinner concept you read under "How to Express the SECRET POWER Inside of Your Creative Moment," and turn it into a date with your spouse. Create a posh international dinner date. Cook a dish from different parts of the world and lay it out like a buffet. Have music and flags hanging from those different places for atmosphere.

Brooke's 101 Top Secrets

If you do not have the time to cook or know how to cook, go out to the restaurants from different parts of the world, for example: go to a French restaurant then go to a Mexican restaurant for drinks, and then to a Japanese restaurant to have sushi. Do this all in one night!

59. Do something small for seven days before your spouse's birthday, for example:

Your Wife's Birth Date

February 1st - Decorate the bathroom (when she wakes up to get ready for work she will be surprised).

February 2nd - Send flowers to her job.

February 3rd – Schedule a masseuse to come to the house to give your wife a massage.

February 4th - Prepare breakfast.

February 5th - Take her to get an outfit.

February 6th - Organize a surprise birthday party the day before her birthday.

That will really be a surprise!

February 7th (On Her Birthday) - Go out to dinner and talk about the whole week. ☺

60. Purchase an old fashion laundry basket, an old fashion clothes line, and clothes pin. On each clothes pin clip a pair of boxers. Fill up the entire

clothes line. Then fold the line in the laundry basket. When he pulls it out the long clothes line will stretch so long with nothing but his favorite under clothes. It's really nice when someone pulls one end while someone has the other end of the clothes line and stretches it until the line ends.

61. Prepare a tantalizing *Breakfast in Bed* for your spouse, except the food on the tray is for you to be creative and to dine from your spouse's body.

62. Have a picnic in your living room and ask your spouse to join you. The picnic basket should be full of edible X-rated naughty alluring treats. Yum!

Job & Home-Based Ideas

63. Start a Pet and Animal Business

64. Charge up to $150.00/Hour with Your Business-to Business Services

65. Earn Up to $100,000 in a 24-hour Child Care Business

66. Earn Up to $100,000 in the Computer and Internet Business

67. Earn Up to $80,000 in Environmental and Green Business

68. Become a Sonographer

69. Manage Singers, Actors, or Models

70. Grow a Vegetable or Fruit Garden in Your Backyard and Sell it to Your Neighborhood

71. Earn Up to $65,000 in Health-Related Businesses

72. Sell Keepsake Dream Boxes

73. Make Money with Baby Boomer and Senior Services

74. $500/Week Operating a Laundry Service

75. Become a Mystery Shopper

76. Sell Fancy Friendship Bracelets Made Out of Bamboo Twig or Fabric

77. Teach Ways in How to Create Memorable and Persuasive Presentations

78. Teach Ways to Add Value to Real Estate

79. Start a Craft Business and Sell it on www.Etsy.com

80. Earn up to $40,000 in the Honey, Jams and Jellies Business

81. Become a Fashion Model or Actor

82. Write Successful Grab'em Fast Unforgettable Press Releases for Clients

83. Run Errands for the Elderly

More Ways to Make Money

84. Start Your Own Dish Washing Service

85. If You Have a Curly Willow Tree or Manzanita Thicket Trim, Dry, and Sell to Local Florists or Craftspeople – Pine Cones and Mistletoe Are Great as Well

86. Become a Dog Walker

87. Working on a Project and Need Funding? Sign-up for www.Indiegogo.com or www.Kickstarter.com

88. Rent Out Your Unused Parking Spot, Driveway, or Spare Room

89. Learn How to Make and Sell Intriguing Jewelry

90. Earn Money in the Martial Art Business by Developing an After-School Program

91. Sell Your Pristine Hair

92. Earn Money Selling Adorable Baby Clothing and Accessories

Opportunities for Children to Earn Money

93. Set up a Stand and Sell Lemonade or Popsicles

94. Walk Your Neighbor's Dog

95. Organize a Bike & Car Wash Event

96. Mow Your Neighbor's Lawn or Shovel Snow

97. Sell Home Crafts Door-to-Door or Online

98. Babysit the Neighbor's Pets When They Leave for Vacation

99. Clean Your Neighbor's House and Recycle their Bottles, Newspapers, and Cans

100. Produce a Theatrical Play in Your Backyard and Charge an Admission Fee

101. Create a Guide About Your Own 101 Top Secrets

Bonus: Money Secrets

We all want to make money and each of you can make money through the 101 ideas above, but below are the real secrets to making money. Before you read the secrets the common dominator to practicing each secret is having good character. We can make all the money in the world but if we don't have character we could lose the money we made real fast. How? Through excessive spending, which leads to downsizing or even bankruptcy. Here is a list of money secrets you may want to practice so you will not only make money but know how to keep it and be wealthy.

- Put attention on money and money will put attention on you.

- Don't be selfish with money.

- *Spend money to improve the quality of your life.*
- If you don't master the gift of saving, you are destined not to have money.
- To master the profession of money making is to first help others make money.
- Don't do things for money; first find what you love to do then money will come along as a result of that.
- Money is a good tool if you know how to use it.
- How to make serious money is to first increase the value of the product or service.
- One of the biggest pleasures of life is sharing.
- Use other people's money (OPM) to invest until you can do it yourself.
- Serve, teach, and help others and God will supernaturally help you.

Follow Your Bliss

Decorating Tips

Now I know you are thinking, what do decorating tips have to do with making money? Well we want to have a relaxing and peaceful environment to feel good about ourselves and take away the stress while you are making money. Here are some tips:

- Turn your closet into an office by removing the door and putting up a beautiful curtain. Place your desk, chair, office supplies, and work in the closet.

- Use nice jars for q-tips, cotton balls, and sponges. Place it in your bathroom.

Make your own tea bags but instead of using herbs use potpourri and hang the bags from the ceiling to create a well scented enchanting environment.

How to Fulfill Your Purpose...

Would you like to learn more about each idea mentioned in this guide? Do you need a jumpstart with resources to get ahead of the game? Do you need a one-page business proposal or a marketing deck? If the answer is yes to any of these questions, then please attend *Brooke's 101 Top Secret Bootcamp Sponsored by BusyB.Global*!

To find out about Brooke's additional products and events please visit www.BusyB.Global

Space is Limited!

BROOKE'S 101 TOP SECRETS

www.BusyB.Global